A Book of Music

A Book of Music
Jack Spicer

Improvisations On A Sentence By Poe

"Indefiniteness is an element of the true music."
The grand concord of what
Does not stoop to definition. The seagull
Alone on the pier cawing its head off
Over no fish, no other seagull,
No ocean. As absolutely devoid of meaning
As a French horn.
It is not even an orchestra. Concord
Alone on a pier. The grand concord of what
Does not stoop to definition. No fish
No other seagull, no ocean—the true
Music.

A Valentine

Useless Valentines
Are better
Than all others.
Like something implicit
In a poem.
Take all your Valentines
And I'll take mine.
What is left is better
Than any image.

Cantata

Ridiculous
How the space between three violins
Can threaten all of our poetry.
We bunch together like Cub
Scouts at a picnic. There is a high scream.
Rain threatens. That moment of terror.
Strange how all our beliefs
Disappear.

Orfeo

Sharp as an arrow Orpheus
Points his music downward.
Hell is there
At the bottom of the seacliff.
Heal
Nothing by this music.
Eurydice
Is a frigate bird or a rock or some seaweed.
Hail nothing
The infernal
Is a slippering wetness out at the horizon.
Hell is this:
The lack of anything but eternal to look at
The expansiveness of salt
The lack of any bed but one's
Music to sleep in.

Song Of A Prisoner

Nothing in my body escapes me.
The sound of an eagle diving
Upon some black bird
Or the sorrow of an owl.
Nothing in my body escapes me.
Each branch is closed
I
Echo each song from its throat
Bellow each sound.

Jungle Warfare

The town wasn't much
A few mud-huts and a church steeple.
They were the same leaves
And the same grass
And the same birds deep in the edge of the thicket.
We waited around for someone to come out and surrender
But they rang their church bells
And we
We were not afraid of death or any manner of dying
But the same muddy bullets, the same horrible
Love.

Good Friday: For Lack Of An Orchestra

I saw a headless she-mule
Running through the rain
She had the hide of a chessboard
And withers that were lank and dark
"Tell me," I asked
"Where
Is Babylon?"
"No," she bellowed
"Babylon is a few baked bricks
With some symbols on them.
You could not hear them. I am running
To the end of the world."
She ran
Like a green and purple parrot, screaming
Through the sand.

Mummer

The word is imitative
From the sound mum or mom
Used by nurses to frighten or amuse children
At the same time pretending
To cover their faces.
Understanding is not enough
The old seagull died. There is a whole army of seagulls
Waiting in the wings
A whole army of seagulls.

The Cardplayers

The moon is tied to a few strings
They hold in their hands. The cardplayers
Sit there stiff, hieratic
Moving their hands only for the sake of
Playing the cards.
No trick or metaphor
Each finger is a real finger
Each card real pasteboard, each liberty
Unaware of attachment.
The moon is tied to a few strings.

                              Those cardplayers

Stiff, utterly
Unmoving.

Ghost Song

The in
       ability to love
The inability
            to love
In love
       (like all the small animals went up the hill into the
       underbrush to escape from the goat and the bad tiger)
The inability
Inability
       (tell me why no white flame comes up from the earth
       when lightning strikes the twigs and the dry branches)
In love. In love. In love. The
In-
  ability
       (as if there were nothing left on the mountains but
       what nobody wanted to escape from)

Army Beach With Trumpets

Rather than our bodies the sand
Proclaims that we are on the last edge
Of something. Two boys
Who cannot catch footballs horseplay
On the wet edge.
Or if the sight of the thing ended
Did not break upon us like a wave
From every warm ocean.
We call it sport
To play on the edge, to drop
Like a heartless football
At the edge.

Duet For A Chair And A Table

The sounds of words as they fall away from our mouths
Nothing
Is less important
And yet that chair
              this table
                    named
Assume identities
                    take their places
Almost as a kind of music.
Words make things name
                themselves
Makes the table grumble

                    I

In the symphony of God am a table
Makes the chair sing
A little song about the people that will never be sitting on it
And we
Who in the same music
Are almost as easily shifted as furniture
We
Can learn our names from our mouths
Name our names
In the middle of the same music.

Conspiracy

A violin which is following me

In how many distant cities are they listening
To its slack-jawed music? This
Slack-jawed music?
Each of ten thousand people playing it.

Oh, my heart would sooner die
Than leave its slack-jawed music. They
In those other cities
Whose hearts would sooner die.

It follows me like someone that hates me.

Or is it really a tree growing just behind my throat
That if I turned quickly enough I could see
Rooted, immutable, neighboring
Music.

A Book Of Music

Coming at the end, the lovers
Are exhausted like two swimmers. Where
Did it end? There is no telling. No love is
Like an ocean with the dizzy procession of the waves'
      boundaries
From which two can emerge exhausted, nor long goodbye
Like death.
Coming at an end. Rather, I would say, like a length
Of coiled rope
Which does not disguise in the final twists of its lengths
Its endings.
But, you will say, we loved
And some parts of us loved
And the rest of us will remain
Two persons. Yes,
Poetry ends like a rope.

'A Book of Music' by Jack Spicer

© 1958, 2023 The Estate of Jack Spicer

Originally published in 1969 by White Rabbit Press

Published in 2023 by Pilot Press

978-1-7393649-0-8